ye his Saints:

an Anthology of excerpts from the Psalms and Gospels

with illustrations of crosses, sites and buildings
associated with Scotland's Saints,
and commentary on their lives and legends.

1

First published in November 2004
by Kildalton Press,
Inverness IV2 3XP

ISBN: 0-9549033-0-7

Printed and bound in Great Britain
by Dingwall Printers Limited, Dingwall, Ross-shire IV15 9UG

In memory
of
my parents
and
all the saints
who from their labours rest

and
with grateful thanks to
my wife,
with whom I travelled to all the sites
written about and illustrated within,
for all her help and encouragement.

Kildalton   Cross, Islay.

FOREWORD

I am privileged, indeed, to introduce this remarkable book and I do so with the greatest pleasure. The concept of linking excerpts from the Psalms and the Gospels to the lives of Scotland's saints and the places where they lived is inspired. The Psalms, in particular, have always been at the centre of worship in Scotland.

Allan Haldane and his wife Dorothy travelled all over the country visiting the places associated with the Saints, so that the illustrations of crosses, chapels, gravestones were made directly at the sites. The scholarly accounts of the lives and works of these Saints also include the legends, which were loved by the people of the time. These legends, as Allan says, are often nearer to the truth than historical accounts. The Saints were human beings, living frugally, in close touch with nature, perhaps early conservationists. In these pages they come very much alive.

Saint Columba was known as "the dove", but also as "the wolf". He had his moments of anger as well as his many expressions of mercy and love.

Did Saint Margaret, in her enthusiasm for the teachings of Rome, did she, as Allan puts it, *"preside over the demise of Columba's Celtic Church?"*

In this book, the poetry of the Old and the New Testaments is reflected in the exquisite beauty of the illustrations. This is a book to treasure and to return to again and again.

Katharine Stewart.

Katharine Stewart, author of *A Croft in the Hills*
and other books on Highland life.

CONTENTS

PREFACE

Psalm 34

8. O taste and see that the LORD is good:
blessed is the man that trusteth in him.
9. O fear the LORD, ye his saints:
for there is no want in them that fear him.
10. The young lions do lack, and suffer hunger:
But they that seek the LORD shall not want any good thing.

King James Authorised Version.

In Chapter XXIII in the third book of St Adamnan's *Life of St Columba* it is written of Columba that *"coming down from the knoll and returning to the monastery, he sat in his hut transcribing the Psalter; and coming to that verse of the thirty third Psalm (in the Vulgate) where it is written 'But they that seek the LORD shall not want any good thing.' 'Here,' he says, 'I must stop at the foot of the page and what follows let Baithene write.'"*

After transcribing the verse, attending Church for vesper mass of the vigil of the Lord's Day, and returning to his cell, where he had bare rock for pallet and a stone for pillow, he sits up through the night. And there, sitting up, he gives his last commands to the Brethren.

"After which," writes Adamnan, *"as the last happy hour gradually approached, the Saint was silent. Then when the bell began to toll midnight, rising in haste he goes to the Church, and running faster than the others he enters alone, and on bended knee he falls down in prayer at the altar. Finally, with wonderful cheerfulness and joy of countenance, on seeing the holy angels coming to meet him,"* he gives his blessing to the Brethren and *"after signifying his holy benediction, immediately breathed forth his spirit."*

So died the first abbot of Iona, on 9th June AD 597. He had first arrived there in AD 563, two hundred years after St Ninian had founded Candida Casa on the shores of the Solway and in the same year that St Augustine landed among the Saxons of Kent.

Opposite: Looking across the Sound of Iona to the island of Mull from the slopes of Tor an Aba. Tor an Aba, or the Abbott's Knoll, is the hilly outcrop of rock where it is believed Columba had his wooden writing hut. From there he could see over the sound to Mull of the Bens and over all that he, as Abbot, was in charge of. He is even reputed to have been heard on the distant shores of Mull issuing commands to the brethren on Iona!

The restored Abbot's House belonging to the Benedictine Order of the 13th century can be seen in the foreground. It is part of the restoration of the Abbey and monastery started in the early 20th century by the Iona Cathedral Trust and completed by the Iona Community in the mid 20th century. Alongside the Abbot's House are the Abbey gardens and beyond that the remaining one wall of the Bishop's House, Tigh an Easbuig, thought to have been built in the 1630s.

INTRODUCTION

In compiling the text for this volume, I have followed the example of many of Scotland's saints who took great delight in transcribing excerpts from the Psalms and Gospels. Masterpieces such as the *Book of Kells* and the *Book of Durrow* were created by them. The *Book of Kells* was probably started or completed on Iona before being removed to Kells in Ireland for safe keeping when Iona was subjected to repeated raids by the Vikings. St Columba's remains were likewise removed to Ireland for safekeeping at that time.

As well as recording excerpts from the Psalms and the Gospels I have retold some intriguing stories handed down through the ages concerning these Saints. I offer no guarantee of historical authenticity but what is authentic, I am sure, is that these stories took hold in the minds of those who revered the saints and that they were greatly influenced by them.

In the Museum of Scotland in Edinburgh one can view the Monymusk Relic (also known as the Brec Bennoch) probably dating from the 8th century, a casket containing, legend has it, the relics of Saint Columba. Like the relics of Saint Andrew brought to these shores by Regulus, it played an important part in the lives of Scotland's Church and Royalty in the Middle Ages.

Today the Vatican divides relics into two classes, a division that has nothing to do with the authenticity of the relic. The difference lies in whether the relic is an actual fragment of a saint's body, in which case it is a first-class relic, or something which has been touched by a saint, which is classified as a second-class relic.

In the Middle Ages, great stress was laid on possessing such relics. Interestingly, the late Professor Barclay, of Glasgow University, declares that true Christians have no need for relics. They can avail themselves of much more authentic and valuable relics in the actual words and teachings of our Lord himself as found in the Gospels. Such relics would surely be classified as first-class, giving us a direct insight into the heart and mind of Jesus and in so doing, in his words *"seeing the Father"*.

Jesus was steeped in Scripture and in this respect the Psalms could be considered as second-class relics as they were read and their teachings totally absorbed by our Lord. Jesus quoted from the Psalms and used the imagery of the Psalms in much of his teaching. Praise or prayer, the Psalmist delights in the goodness and greatness of God but sometimes doubts the presence of God at the moment of greatest need. The Psalms, too, could surely be considered as first-class relics giving us, as they do, direct access to the Psalmist's inmost thoughts and letting us share in his despair, his hopes and in his moments of great joy.

The accompanying illustrations are of crosses, sites and buildings, some in ruins, some restored and some modern, all of which are associated with or dedicated to the Saints. This anthology is not intended to be a religious thesis but rather the whole should act as a stimulus to reflection and contemplation of the Word and of the lives of the Saints.

St Matthew's Gospel Chapter 7.

7. Ask and it shall be given you; seek and ye shall find: knock, and it shall be opened unto you:

8. For every one that asketh receiveth; and he that seeketh findeth; and to him that knocketh it shall be opened.

11. If ye then, being evil, know how to give good gifts unto your children, how much more will your Father which is in heaven give good things to them that ask him.

King James Authorised Version.

The best-known St Clement was martyred in AD 100. He was a disciple of St Peter and Bishop of Rome. The Romans had him cast into the sea attached to an anchor. Not surprisingly, he became the patron saint of harbour sites and sea traders. Churches dedicated to St Clement can be found along the east coast of Britain tracing his connections with Scandinavian sea-going traders. Dingwall has strong sea-going connections with Scandinavia.

Intriguingly, another St Clement, the first Dominican friar to be brought to Scotland, was made Bishop of Dunblane in 1223. His patron was King Alexander II of Scots, who in 1226 gave Dingwall its Royal Charter, creating it a Royal Burgh. He too could be a candidate to be Dingwall's St Clement.

Opposite: Interior of St Clement's Church in Dingwall, Ross-shire, with its allegorical stained glass window in memory of those who died in the First World War, the laid-up colours of the 4th/5th Battalion of the Seaforth Highlanders and memorial window for a noted local family depicting St Columba and St Margaret.

It is unclear when St Clement became associated with the church in Dingwall; indeed it is also unclear to which St Clement the church is dedicated. It is certain that from 1500 there was a chapel attached to the church dedicated to him. To the north of the present church there lies a large splendidly carved stone with the barely decipherable inscription in Latin around its edges reading *"Here lie in Sanctuary, Paris and Patrick Kemp, wife and son of William Kemp, founder of St Clement's Chapel in 1510."* William Kemp may have been a sea trader.

Psalm 84.

1. How lovely is thy dwelling-place,
   O Lord of hosts, to me!
   The tabernacles of thy grace
   how pleasant, Lord, they be!

2. My thirsty soul longs veh'mently,
   yea faints, thy courts to see:
   My very heart and flesh cry out,
   O living God, for thee.

The Psalms of David in metre.

Much has been made by some scholars of the difference between the Celtic Church and the mother Church in Rome, and of the independence of the former. The fact remains, however, that many of the leaders of the Celtic Church made pilgrimages to Rome. Many indeed remained there for a period of study and some were consecrated as Bishops by the Pope at that time. All returned home to Ireland and Scotland, invigorated and full of missionary zeal. The link with Rome can therefore be traced back to Peter and succeeding Popes such as Clement who was martyred in AD 100.

St Clement was the third Bishop of Rome (Pope) after St Peter. He incurred the wrath of the Roman authorities because of rioting against the Christians in Rome and against Pope Clement in particular. He was banished to the Crimea, there to work alongside convicts in the marble quarries. He found many Christians there and comforted and encouraged them. The only spring of drinking water was six miles off, causing great hardship to the convicts. One day Clement saw a lamb scraping at the ground near the quarry and he took that as a sign that water might be there: dug and found a spring. This was seen as a miraculous act and many conversions to the Christian faith followed. This, however, further outraged the Emperor and he ordered that Clement be tied to an anchor and drowned in the sea.

Opposite: St Clement's Church, Dingwall showing the South side facing the town. The present church building replaced the old kirk condemned by the Presbytery of Dingwall in 1795. Building began in 1800 and was contracted to be completed by 1801. The parish lands of Davidson of Tulloch made up about two thirds of the parish and he, as principal heritor, by law would have to pay most of the cost of a new church. It would seem that he, in collusion with the minister, arranged a plan which would enhance the new approach to Dingwall from his castle. To maintain good relations the presbytery accepted the plan, but confined their approval to the adequacy and accommodation of the new church. This indicated something untoward about the plan, and so there was. The new kirk of Dingwall was to have four large Gothic windows on its south side facing the town, but an expansive Classical false front and steeple on its north side facing Tulloch's castle and giving a pleasing entry to Dingwall from Tulloch's estate. An anchor was recently incorporated into the cobblestone forecourt of the Church in commemoration of the Martyrdom of St Clement in the belief that it was, indeed, that particular St Clement to whom the church is dedicated.

Psalm 24

3. Who shall ascend into the hill of the LORD?
or who shall stand in his holy place?
4. He that hath clean hands, and a pure heart;
who hath not lifted up his soul unto vanity,
nor sworn deceitfully.
5. He shall receive the blessing from the LORD.
and righteousness from the God of his salvation.

King James Authorised Version.

One saint, not of Scotland, but one who influenced the Celtic saints greatly, was St Martin of Tours, in France. It has been said that his life spanned the 4th century like a rainbow. The Roman Empire was doomed but the Church had become an organised and dynamic body prepared to confront and convert the barbarous invaders. That the Church was equipped for this task in Gaul was almost entirely due to St Martin. Born in Central Europe of pagan parents, it was as an officer in the Imperial cavalry that he first went to Gaul. Artists all down the ages felt inspired to paint him leaning from his horse to give his cloak to a shivering beggar. The action reveals the Christian, though when this incident took place he was not yet baptised. However he soon *"flew to be baptised,"* and called upon to engage his enemies in battle, rather than kill them, he faced them unarmed.

Although the battle was never fought, his superiors agreed that this young man would never make a soldier and gave him his freedom. He became a disciple of St Hilary of Poitiers and from him he obtained permission to live as a solitary monk and was given land at Ligugé on which to build his White Hut. The fame of his miracles and of his great sanctity soon drew to him a host of visitors. Those visitors persuaded him to turn his hut into a monastic *'White House'*, which became a model throughout Gaul, Britain and Ireland for similar settlements. One of these visitors was Scotland's St Ninian who chose to call his settlement at Whithorn, Candida Casa or White House.

We owe it to the pen of Sulpicius Severus, St Martin's biographer, that we catch a glimpse of the great mystic evangelist who moulded St Ninian and who spent many years preparing Gaul to meet the Teutonic invaders. The collapse of the Empire failed to stem the world-wide flow of pilgrims to his tomb. He writes *"and surely, if there be dwellers in the Fortunate Isles and the Arctic regions, they too must have heard of the fame of Martin."*

Opposite: St Martin's Cross on Iona, with Tor an Aba or the Abbot's Knoll in the background. It was sculpted from a single slab of stone sometime between AD 750 and AD 800. The west side is richly carved with biblical scenes while the east side is decorated with bosses and serpents, all reminiscent of contemporary decorative metalwork and manuscripts. St Columba was one of many who made his pilgrimage to the Saint's tomb in Tours.

St Matthew's Gospel Chapter 5

6. Blessed are they which do hunger and thirst
after righteousness:
for they shall be filled.

7. Blessed are the merciful: for they shall obtain mercy.

8. Blessed are the pure in heart for they shall see God.

9. Blessed are the peacemakers:
for they shall be called the children of God.

King James Authorised Version.

If legend speaks truly of St Ninian, he had a great advantage over foreign missionaries among the Britons of Strathclyde in the 5th century as he was one of themselves and the son of a man of note. According to tradition he was born somewhere in the area of the Solway Firth. Roman Britain, south of Hadrian's Wall, was officially Christian and according to Aelred, writing in the 12th century, Ninian learnt not only the elements of a Latin education but the rudiments of the Christian faith. *"His soul was hot within him with zeal for perfection in all things of holy religion and he longed for instruction which would enable him to become a worthy minister of Jesus Christ."* Accordingly, he left home and went to Rome. He was ordained as a priest and persuaded after a while to undertake the task of carrying the Gospel to his own people. By way of Tours, where he stayed as an earnest pupil of Martin, he made his way, by sea, to the shores of the Solway Firth, to Whithorn in Galloway. In his monastery in Whithorn, which he called Candida Casa, he established a school where young men and probably women were instructed in Christian doctrine before being sent to carry the faith to the Picts, Britons and Scots of Alba and Ireland.

One of the greatest and the most famous of Ninian's pupils at Candida Casa was a young man named Patrick. He was, in all probability, born in Strathcyde, near Dumbarton about AD 387. Captured by raiders from Ireland as a lad, he worked in Ulster as a house slave for ten years before escaping back to Scotland. He came under the influence of Ninian, became a student at Candida Casa and returned to Ireland spreading the Gospel among the pagans of the land where he had once been a slave. He is now remembered as St Patrick, patron and protector of that land.

St Ninian died about the year AD 423. If any man earned the title *'apostle of Scotland'*, it was he. Ninian founded many churches throughout what was to become Scotland, the most notable of them being Glasgow. It is said that he even reached the shores of the Pentland Firth and the Northern Isles.

Opposite: Isle of Whithorn is a picturesque harbour village on the shores of the Solway and one which has been no stranger to tragedy in recent years. Tradition has it that Ninian landed here after his sojourn in Rome and France. There is a ruined 13th century church on the shore but pictured here is the present day church. The larger cross in the inset is one of many in the Museum in Whithorn dating from the 10th century, made in Whithorn by one of a school of sculptors. Also illustrated is an earlier cross, found at Kirkmadrine, with the Chi Rho symbol (X and R being, in Greek, the first two letters of Christ) encircled by what some say is a ring of glory and others a circle representing eternity, dating from pagan times. It developed into what we know as the Celtic wheel cross.

Psalm 37.

8. Cease from anger, and forsake wrath:
fret not thyself in any wise to do evil.
9. For evildoers shall be cut off:
but those that wait upon the LORD,
they shall inherit the earth.
11. But the meek shall inherit the earth;
and shall delight themselves in the abundance of peace.

King James Authorised Version.

The histories of the Celtic saints constantly mention their staffs and little hand-bells. At least one staff and several bells have survived to this day. The fact that St Ninian's staff was held in reverence is illustrated by the following story related by Aelred, Ninian's biographer. *"Both nobles and men of middle rank"* he writes *"trusted their sons to the blessed pontiff to be trained in sacred learning. He indoctrinated these by his knowledge, curbing by a salutary discipline the vices to which their age was prone, and persuasively inculcating the virtues whereby they might live soberly, righteously and piously."*

Having committed a misdemeanour which didn't escape the Saint's notice and one which demanded punishment, one young student fled in terror but *"not being ignorant of the power of the holy man,"* writes Aelred, *"he was careful to carry away with him the staff on which Ninian used to lean, thinking that he had procured the best comfort for the journey, by taking anything which belonged to the saint."* Finding a coracle but one which, unfortunately, had no outer skin, he set out to sea. In minutes water poured in through the open holes in the craft. Praying for divine guidance and trusting in the powers of the holy man, he stuck the staff into one of the holes. At once the water ceased to enter the craft and *"the staff, acting for sail, caught the wind; the staff as helm directed the vessel; the staff as anchor stayed it."* To the amazement of onlookers, the boy floated back to the shore and safety. And perhaps to chastisement?

Much of the Christian missionary work started in Scotland by Ninian and his followers was undone when the Roman occupation of Britain ended and, in place of the cultured Romans, crude aggressive Saxons invaded Southern Scotland. Great numbers of converts lapsed into paganism but Ninian's own church and work survived and his message of love flared up in another place. In Ireland, churchmen who had studied at Candida Casa established monasteries there. One in particular was Finnian, who had a student whose name would become synonymous with Christianity in Scotland when he, in turn came to these shores. His name was Columba.

Opposite: Norman arch in the nave of the ruined 12th century Priory at Whithorn on the site of St Ninian's Candida Casa, his first church and foundation in Scotland, established in AD 397. Excavations have revealed that Ninian's church was indeed white, inside and out. It was called after St Martin's hut at Ligugé. The word 'white' was initially used, apparently, as synonymous with holy.

St Matthew's Gospel Chapter 5

3. Blessed are the poor in spirit: for their's is the kingdom of heaven.
4. Blessed are they that mourn: for they shall be comforted.
5. Blessed are the meek: for they shall inherit the earth.

King James Authorised Version.

Columba was born on a Thursday, known in the Islands as the *'Day of Columba benign'*, a good day to be starting a venture and one which many couples consider to be a lucky day to be wed. He was born in Donegal in AD 521, his father being a Clan chieftain. His mother was of royal blood. He was christened Colum (dove) and Crimthain (wolf). His parents decided that their son should aim to become a priestly scholar and while in foster care, which was the tradition, he became imbued with deeply religious feelings and received the name Colum-kill or Colum of the cell. At Clonard he was ordained a priest but he also learned how to plough and sow and reap, how to build both boat and house, and he acquired a taste for music and poetry while also being a robust sportsman. He established many churches and monasteries but it would appear that on many occasions the wolf in him overcame the dove as he had an imperious temper.

One of his former tutors was Finnian, who, on returning to Ireland from Rome with a new translation of the Gospels by St Jerome, loaned it to Columba for him to study. Columba copied it for his own use. When Finnian found out, he was furious and took Columba to court. They appeared before Dairmait, High King of Ireland, at Tara and Dairmait found in favour of Finnian, famously declaring *"to every cow belongeth her calf"* and by implication *"to every book belongeth its copy."* Columba was now the furious one, but with Dairmait rather than Finnian, and vowed to be avenged in battle. It may be that Columba was angry with Dairmait for another reason. Dairmait had caused the death of a kinsman of Columba, the young prince Curnan, who had taken refuge with him. For whatever reason, battle commenced and Dairmait's army was defeated by Columba's kinsmen, the Clan O'Neill. It was said that Columba himself had mustered them. His standing as a religious leader was greatly compromised and his brother clerics sat in judgement over him, accusing him of encouraging his followers to kill 3000 of the King's men. Columba imposed sentence on himself, of exile, and sailed across the seas to Scotland vowing to win as many souls for Christ as had fallen in battle. The Dove was emerging as victor over the Wolf.

Opposite: St Columba's Chapel, Southend, Kintyre. In Kintyre the belief exists that rather than sailing to Oronsay, then to Iona, Columba took the short sea crossing to Kintyre, landing at Keil in Southend. He then progressed up through the Kintyre peninsula before crossing to the isles. The ruined chapel at Southend bears his name, though of a later date. Nearby can be found St Columba's footsteps. These footsteps, one of which pre-dates Columba by probably 1000 years, were carved into the rock and, according to tradition, on the death of an old chief the new chief would swear faithfulness to his tribe while facing East with his foot placed in the carved step. Mindful of such a tradition, it is believed that Columba did likewise, thus declaring himself to be a new kind of chief.

St Matthew's Gospel Chapter 5

14. Ye are the light of the world.
A city that is set on a hill cannot be hid.
15. Neither do men light a candle,
and put it under a bushel, but on a candlestick;
and it giveth light to all that are in the house.
16. Let your light so shine before men,
that they may see your good works,
and glorify your father which is in heaven.

King James Authorised Version

There is in Iona a little bay, with shingle beach, which indents its southern shore: Port na Churraich, the Bay of the Coracle. It was here that Columba landed in AD 563 with twelve companions. A near-by hill is called Carn cul ri Erin, *'the Cairn of the Back turned to Ireland'*, marking the spot where the exile found that his beloved Ireland could no longer be discerned on the horizon. At the northern-most point of the island there is Traigh an t-suidhe, *'the Shore of the Seat'*, a favourite resting place of the saint. Tor an Aba, *'the Abbot's Knoll'*, (a small hill near the Abbey) is yet another name on this island associated with its first abbot, Columba. On his last evening he climbed this knoll, blessed Iona and declared that it would be much honoured in years to come, which indeed it has been. In its early days the monastic community attained great stature and its missionaries, Columba included, spread the Christian message to the farthest corners of Pictland in the north and as far as Northumbria in the south.

Religion, the written word, art and politics were for Columba inextricably mixed. He was not blind to the possibilities inherent in political alliances and was reputed to be a king maker. He confronted a potential enemy in King Brude of the Picts whose allegiance he won. One could claim that Columba was responsible for the unification of Picts and Scots, which in time led to the creation of the nation of Scotland as we know it today.

Opposite: St Martin's Cross outside Iona Abbey with a replica of St John's Cross casting its shadow on the little building known as St Columba's Shrine built where, it is believed, the saint was first laid to rest. These crosses were, in all probability, used as visual aids by the monks when preaching to an illiterate audience, with their large carved biblical images and interlaced decoration. There were, at one time, many of these crosses on Iona but like the St John's Cross they have suffered from the ravages of the weather and the invading pagan hordes.

Psalm 145

9. The LORD is good to all:
and his tender mercies are over all his works.
10. All thy works shall praise thee, O LORD;
and thy saints shall bless thee.
11. They shall speak of the glory of thy kingdom,
and talk of thy power;
12. To make known to the sons of men his mighty acts,
and the glorious majesty of his kingdom.

King James Authorised Version

It has been suggested that, in order to secure the right to ordain a new king of Dalriada, St Adamnan, in his *Life of St Columba*, invented the story that that saint had ordained and anointed King Aedan.

Adamnan was the ninth Abbot of Iona and a successor to Columba, and his biography of the Saint was widely read. The inauguration ceremony, invented or true, was copied by at least one foreign monarchy. In his *Life* he divided his work into three books, the first dealing with the Prophetic revelations of the Saint, the second with his Divine Miracles and the third with Angelic Visitations. It is less a biography than a hagiography, being short on many aspects of St Columba's life. Many of Adamnan's works were equally influential and one in particular is quite remarkable. In AD 697 he produced his 'Law of Innocents' which was an attempt to protect non-combatants, women, children and clerics in time of war. He managed to get the law ratified by the King of Dalriada, the King of the Picts and fifty Irish kings. The works of Adamnan established Iona as a centre of learning despite its position on the fringe of the civilised world. We owe it to his pen that Columba and Iona were, and are, held in such high esteem.

Opposite: The Augustinian Nunnery on Iona. Despite repeated attacks by Vikings, the monastery on Iona survived and around 1200 further building took place. A Benedictine Abbey replaced the old Columban monastery and an Augustinian Nunnery was built at a discreet distance from it. The Reformation in Scotland in the 16th century put an end to the monastic life on Iona and both the Abbey and Nunnery fell into picturesque disrepair. In 1899 the eighth Duke of Argyll, who owned the entire island, transferred ownership of the Abbey, Reilig Odhráin, and the Nunnery to a newly established Iona Cathedral Trust. The Trust had to raise every penny of the funds needed to restore the buildings and by 1902 work was underway. Work on the nave was completed in 1910. In 1938, with the establishment of the Iona Community by the Reverend George F. Macleod, a new era in the rebirth of the Abbey began. He brought together trainee ministers and craftsmen to commence the work of rebuilding, and the Abbey was completed in 1965. All are now in the care of Historic Scotland.

Psalm 8

4. What is man that thou art mindful of him?
and the Son of man, that thou visiteth him?
5. For thou hast made him a little lower than the angels,
and hast crowned him with glory and honour.
6. Thou madest him to have dominion over the works of thy hand;
thou hast put all things under his feet :
7. All sheep and oxen, yea, and the beasts of the field;
8. The fowl of the air and the fish of the sea,
and whatsoever passeth through the paths of the sea.

King James Authorised Version

"When the blessed man was sojourning for some days in the province of the Picts, he was obliged to cross the river Nesa (Ness); and when he had come to the bank, he sees some of the inhabitants burying an unfortunate fellow, whom as those who were burying him related, a little while before some aquatic monster seized and savagely bit while he was swimming." So the story is told by Adamnan in his *Life of St Columba,* Chapter XXVII of the Second Book. Adamnan goes on to tell how the unfortunate man's companions had tried to save him but to no avail. Columba, on hearing the story, ordered one of his companions to swim out and bring over a coble which was berthed on the other bank. The companion immediately cast off all but his tunic and cast himself into the water, but *"the monster suddenly comes up and moves towards the man as he swam in mid stream, and with a great roar rushes on him with open mouth, while all who were there, barbarians as well as Brethren, were greatly terror-struck. The blessed man seeing it, after making the Salutory Sign of the Cross, commanded the ferocious monster, saying: 'Go thou no further, nor touch the man; go back at once.' Then on hearing the word of the Saint, the monster was terrified and fled away."*

The Brethren greatly marvelled that their comrade had returned to them unharmed and glorified God. *"And even the barbarous heathens who were present, constrained by the greatness of the miracle which they themselves had seen, magnified the God of the Christian."*

Opposite: St Columba's Roman Catholic Cathedral in Oban. Bishop Martin cut the first sod for the foundation of the new cathedral in 1932, on the site of an older church built in 1886. The building was completed in 1934 and was designed by Sir Giles Gilbert Scott, the celebrated architect who designed Liverpool's Anglican cathedral and the famous red telephone kiosk! It is the seat of the Bishop of Argyll and the Isles. The lectern falls were created by Margaret Maclellan of Fort William in 1997 to commemorate the 1400th anniversary of St Columba's death.

St Matthew's Gospel, Chapter 6.

25. Therefore I say unto you, Take no thought for your life, what ye shall eat, or what ye shall drink; nor yet for your body, what ye shall put on. Is not life more than meat, and the body than raiment?

26. Behold the fowls of the air: for they sow not, neither do they reap, nor gather into barns; yet your heavenly Father feedeth them. Are ye not much better than they?

Chapter 8.

20. Foxes have holes and the birds of the air have nests; but the Son of man hath not where to lay his head.

King James Authorised Version.

St Ciaran, founder of Clonmacnoise in Western Ireland, prophesied, as did his friend and contemporary St Columba, that a disaster would befall the world of the Celts. He begged those who should pray to him after his death to *"hasten to other places and leave my remains just like the dry bones of the stag on the mountain: for it is better that you should be with my spirit in heaven than alongside my bones on earth with scandal."* This didn't stop 9th century clerics making tremendous efforts to preserve the bodies of their beloved saints from pollution, St Columba's remains having been taken across the Irish Channel to another resting place as the Viking hordes invaded the western seaboard of Scotland and Ireland itself. St Ciaran's predicted disaster was upon the Celtic world.

Like many of the Celtic saints St Ciaran had a great affinity with animals. It is said that a fox had been his companion in childhood and that while he studied under Finnian at Clonard he would rest his book on the antlers of a tame stag. He it was who established the great abbey of Clonmacnoise on the banks of the Shannon. When on Aran Island he dreamed of a great fruit tree overlooking a river, and surely Clonmacnoise was the realisation of that dream as it became one of the great schools of Europe. In Ireland it was second only to Armagh as a centre of literature and art.

It would appear that Ciaran undertook missionary journeys to Scotland and worked mainly in Kintyre. Several sites are dedicated to him, including one in Islay – Kilchiaran – which dates from the 14th century.

Opposite: St Ciaran's Church of Scotland at Achnacarry, Lochaber on the estate of Cameron of Lochiel. Built as a mission church in 1908 to serve the surrounding area, it housed a moving ecumenical service for the 2001 International Rally of Clan Cameron with clansmen and women from around the globe attending in the presence of their 91-year-old chief, Lochiel, and his family.

Salm XXXIV

10. Bidh easbhuidh air na leòmhanaibh òga,
agus bith ocras orra;
ach orra-san a dh'iarras an Tighearna
cha bhi maith air bith a dìth.
11. Thigibh, a chlann, éisdibh rium:
teagaisgidh mi dhuibh eagal an Tighearna.

Biobull Gaidhlig Alba.
The Bible in Gaelic.

Both St Columba and St Kentigern (perhaps better known as St Mungo) could be referred to as ecclesiastical statesmen. They met once, to exchange staffs, which in the Celtic Church signified the ratification of some important agreement. Kentigern had been consecrated bishop of the Church of the Britons in Strathclyde and established his seat where Glasgow now is. He became a friend and confidant of St David, a fellow Briton working in Wales, and both men were deeply concerned about the encroachment into their territories by the invading Angles. The Angles, however, were not the only encroaching influence. Aeden, from his capital Dunadd, in Dalriada, planned raids that gained for the Scots the whole of Argyllshire and north west Scotland, and he even penetrated into Brude's Pictland. In all of these expansionist thrusts he was apparently encouraged by Columba. One of these campaigns saw the establishment of a Columban settlement at Drymen in Strathclyde, and protests were made to Columba by Kentigern concerning these incursions into British territory. Hence the reason for an elaborately arranged summit meeting of the two clerics on the banks of the Molindinar, which flows into the Clyde where the city of Glasgow (whose patron saint is St Kentigern or St Mungo) now stands.

Joceline, a well-known 12th century hagiographer, tells us in his Life of St Kentigern that the two saints approached each other, preceded by members of their respective parties singing psalms. When the two godfearing men met they embraced and kissed each other. The two began discussions, Columba of Iona and Mungo, the faithful watchdog of the British Church. Each put forward his view amicably, agreement was reached and staffs exchanged. The friendly mood was perhaps aided by the setting. They talked and picnicked by the Molindinar, surrounded by the birds and beasts they loved so much and who were their constant friends.

Opposite: Interior of St Columba's Cathedral, Oban. On the rear wall are two carved wooden panels on either side of the cross, the one on the left depicting Columba meeting King Brude and the one on the right depicting the meeting and exchanging of staffs between St Columba and St Kentigern. The altar cloth bears the paraphrased verse from Psalm 34 (verse 10, above) in Gaelic, which Columba had been writing on the evening of his death: *"cha bhith dith orrasan a shireas an Tighearna"* translated as *"they shall not want who stand by the LORD."*

Psalm 84.

3. Behold the sparrow findeth out an house wherein to rest;
The swallow also for herself hath purchased a nest;
Ev'n thine own altars, where she safe
her young ones forth may bring,
O thou almighty Lord of hosts, who art my God and King.

The Psalms of David in metre.

Princess Thenew, the daughter of the King of Lothian, was cast adrift on the Firth of Forth and left to perish. The princess was expecting an illegitimate child, bringing shame to her father, thus causing him to act in such a cruel manner. Miraculously, wind and tide conveyed her to Culross in Fife where the monks, under St Serf, rescued her and where her son, Mungo, was born. Joceline, Mungo's biographer, relates that on first seeing the baby *"the blessed old man was filled with spiritual laughter."* He named him Kentigern but always called him by his pet name, Mungo (Pictish for my dog or my dear one.) The child could not have selected a better foster father.

One of the most attractive inmates of St Serf's monastery was his pet robin. Joceline writes, *"sometimes it was with him when he read or prayed and by the flapping of its wing or the sound of its inarticulate voice, or by some little gesture, it showed its love for him."* One day while the old saint prayed, young Mungo's school fellows *"availing themselves of the absence of the master, began to indulge in play with the aforesaid bird and while they handled it among them, and sought to snatch it from each other, it got destroyed in their hand and its head was torn from its body."* On this, play became sorrow, *"but Mungo took the bird in his hands and putting the head upon the body he signed it with the cross and lifting it up in his hand he said: 'Lord Jesus Christ give back to this bird the breath of life, that thy blessed name be glorified for ever.'"* Miraculously the bird revived and *"in its usual way flew forth with joy to meet the holy man as he returned from Church."*

Opposite: The Dupplin Cross in St Serf's Church in Dunning, Perthshire. St Serf's missionary journeys can be traced by connecting up the sites which bear his name. All are to the north of the Forth, the most westerly dedication being the still complete medieval church in Dunning. Here the saint is credited with slaying a dragon in a spot still called the Dragon's Den. In this church is located a magnificent cross from Dupplin, originally located on a hillside near Forteviot only a few miles to the north. Forteviot is known to be the site of a royal palace in the 9th century. It is in a part of Scotland which became a centre of Christianity and saw the beginnings of a united people. It stands at the crossroads between Pictland and the Kingdom of Scots. On the cross is the figure of a man on horseback, clearly a leader, and the name of the king, Constantine, who reigned in the early 9th century.

The parish served by St Serf's is first recorded soon after 1200. It was probably Gilbert of Strathearn or the Augustinian canons of Inchaffray who built the church which formed the basis for the present building, the Romanesque tower being its most imposing feature. After the Reformation, the church was altered in several ways to adapt it for new forms of worship. Happily it escaped destruction which was the fate of other churches at that time.

St Matthew's Gospel Chapter 6

28. And why take ye thought for raiment?
Consider the lilies of the field, how they grow;
they toil not, neither do they spin:
29. And yet I say unto you,
That even Solomon in all his glory was not arrayed like one of these.
30. Wherefore, if God so clothe the grass of the field,
which to day is, and to morrow is cast into the oven,
shall he not much more clothe you,
O ye of little faith?

King James Authorised Version.

At one time every child brought up in Glasgow would have been acquainted with the rhyme recalling significant events in the life of that city's patron saint, Mungo: *"Here is the bird that never flew. Here is the tree that never grew. Here is the bell that never rang. Here is the fish that never swam."* The bird that never flew, until Mungo performed his miracle; the tree, now an oak, started in the legend as a hazel branch. As a boy Mungo was in charge of the holy fire in the refectory. He fell asleep and the other boys, being envious of him, put out the fire. When he awoke Mungo broke off some frozen branches from a hazel tree and caused them to burst into flames by praying over them. The bell may have been given to him by the Pope. The reference to the fish brings to mind a legend which shows a modern-minded and very understanding, but nonetheless compassionate saint. He came to the rescue of the queen who gave her lover a ring which had been a gift to her from her husband. Her husband, the king, took the ring from the lover when he was sleeping and threw it into the river Clyde. The king then demanded that his queen produce the gift which she, of course, could not do. In distress she appealed to Mungo for help. Mungo's prayers on her behalf were answered when the ring was found in the mouth of a salmon fished from the river!

Mungo left St Serf's care when he was fifteen and trained for ten years under St Fergus in the county of Stirling until St Fergus died. In the company of fellow students he took to the road with their master's body, on a cart pulled by two bulls. On reaching the site of present day Glasgow the weary beasts halted near a burial place once consecrated by St Ninian. Appropriately they buried their master there and Mungo founded a settlement in that "dear green place" which became an island of peace for the refugee Britons in the area. Created head of the church in Strathclyde by the king, Mungo later journeyed to Wales where he became a close friend of St David. In his Welsh monastery he received the call to return to Glasgow. *"My heart is ready, O God, my heart is ready for whatsoever may please thee."* Return to Glasgow he did, and after extensive missionary work in Aberdeenshire he died on 16th January AD 600, by which time *"he was sighing in his soul for heaven."*

Opposite: Glasgow Cathedral and St Mungo's tomb in the Crypt of that Cathedral and the Coat of Arms of Glasgow displayed on a modern lampost, with the symbols associated with various miraculous events in the life of St Mungo, patron saint of that city. Six centuries after St Mungo had been buried on the banks of the Molindinar a stone church was built on the spot. In the 15th century St Mungo's Cathedral was completed in its present form, occupying the same location.

St Luke's Gospel Chapter 6

37. Judge not, and ye shall not be judged.
condemn not, and ye shall not be condemned:
forgive, and ye shall be forgiven.
38. Give and it shall be given unto you;
good measure, pressed down, and shaken together,
and running over, shall men give into your bosom.
For the same measure that ye mete withal
it shall be measured to you again.

King James Authorised Version

If St Columba ceased to trespass on British and Pictish territory, St Moluag, a disciple of St Comgall of Bangor, Co Down, wandered freely among the Scots and then among the Picts of the Eastern seaboard of Scotland. He planted offshoots of St Comgall's church in Mull, Lewis and Skye, working from his base in Lismore. A native of Lismore, the Rev D Carmichael, relates the following story concerning the great rivalry between Columba and Moluag, which was so intense that it would appear that it swamped the saint in both men on at least one occasion.

"St Moluag was sailing towards Lismore when he beheld a boat carrying St Columba and making for Lismore at highest speed. St Columba's craft was the faster. When St Moluag saw that he was likely to be beaten he seized an axe, cut off his little finger, threw it on the beach, some distance away, and cried out, 'My flesh and blood have first possession of the island, and I bless it in the name of the Lord.' St Columba, seeing that he was outwitted, began to invoke various curses on St Moluag's occupation. 'May you have the alder for your firewood,' wished St Columba. 'The Lord will make the alder burn pleasantly,' replied St Moluag."

The curses and rebuffs continued to be exchanged whenever the two met. Fortunately for their immortal souls, their meetings ceased when St Moluag left the islands for the mainland where he followed St Ninian's well-worn path leading to a group of settlements in the East. He finally established himself in Rosemarkie, Ross-shire, where he died in AD 592. A kinsman of Columba, Earnan, may also have travelled to the Black Isle where Kilearnan commemorates his name.

Opposite: The Rosemarkie Pictish cross-slab, dating from the 8th or 9th century. It has crosses on both sides and elaborate and intricate designs, reminiscent of metalwork and illuminated manuscripts. It was rescued from the floor of Rosemarkie Parish Church in 1821 when rebuilding took place. Subsequently repaired, it stood outside the present church until 1980 when, to protect it from further weathering, it was given a new home in nearby Groam House Museum. In the 8th century, the Pictish King Nechtan ordered that the churches in his kingdom conform to Roman usages regarding calculating the date of Easter etc. This recognition of Papal authority is indicated by the presence of churches in nearby Fortrose dedicated to St Peter and shared with St Boniface who was King Nechtan's agent in enforcing this change. It is likely that St Boniface, or Curitan to give him his Gaelic name, was buried in Rosemarkie as well as St Moluag, the Celtic saint who first established a religious settlement there.

Psalm 121

1. I to the hills will lift mine eyes,
from whence doth come mine aid.
2. My safety cometh from the lord,
who heav'n and earth hath made.
3. Thy foot he'll not let slide, nor will
he slumber that thee keeps.
4. Behold he that keeps Israel,
he slumbers not nor sleeps.

Psalms of David in metre

St John's Gospel Chapter 14

Let not your heart be troubled:
ye believe in God, believe also in me.
2. In my father's house are many mansions:
if it were not so, I would have told you.
I go to prepare a place for you.

King James Authorised Version

When St Columba was on his way to meet King Brude of the Picts in Inverness, he was inspired by the Holy Ghost to hasten to the side of Emchath, a Pictish nobleman, who dwelt by the side of Loch Ness at Airchardon (Urquhart), meaning *'by the wood.'* Columba said, according to Adamnan in his Life of St Columba, *"Let us hasten to meet the holy angels who have been sent forth from the highest regions of heaven to bear on high the soul of a certain heathen man, who has preserved his natural goodness through all his life to an extreme old age, and are awaiting our arrival there that we may baptize him before he dies."* This Columba did, and baptized his son also and his whole household.

Opposite: The ruins of Urquhart Castle on the shores of Loch Ness. Once a royal stronghold surrounded on three sides by water, it was fought over and occupied by both the English and Jacobite forces on different occasions. Originally the seat of the Durwards, the Royal doorkeepers in the 13th century, it was latterly given to Clan Grant in the 17th century. The Grants found it too hard to withstand Jacobite attentions and deserted the castle for more comfortable and modern living quarters. They destroyed much of the castle when they left, but its present ruinous state is partly due to locals making use of the stone as building material for their own houses. The discovery of pieces of vitrified rock on the slopes of the summit where the castle now stands would indicate that from the earliest times it was a well-fortified place. The further finding of fragments of a Pictish brooch has led to speculation that Emchath's residence could have been at the same location.

Psalm 121

5. The Lord thee keeps, the Lord thy shade
on thy right hand doth stay:
6. The moon by night thee shall not smite,
nor yet the sun by day.
7. The Lord shall keep thy soul;
he shall preserve thee from all ill.
8. Henceforth thy going out and in
God keep for ever will.

The Psalms of David in metre.

Killianan, near Abriachan, on the shores of Loch Ness, is situated not far from the spot where St Columba reputedly encountered the Loch Ness monster. Columba journeyed up the Great Glen, from Iona to Inverness, to confront King Brude of the Picts in the 6th century. A centre of learning was established here by Columba's disciples with able boys learning Latin and Greek, so that they could follow acts of worship and praise. They learned to read and write in their native language which was akin to Columba's own. They would also have learned the craft of growing plants for food and healing, the first elements of working in wood and stone and the art of illumination. Killianan means the cell of Fianan (some say Adamnan), a monk of the 6th or 7th century. Above the graveyard is a beautiful old stone thought to have been the foundation stone of Finian's cell. A man-made hole in the middle supported the central wooden pole for the roof. This stone, called the Font-Stone, is called by a greater name than Finian's–St Columba's.

Opposite: Included in the montage is an illustration of a sculptured grave slab in the burying ground of Killianan with now barely decipherable markings on it. It was uncovered by volunteers from an Inverness school when cleaning up the burial ground as part of a Highland Village Project in 1970 and 1973. The stone is noted in the Proceedings of the Society of Antiquaries of Scotland. The incised design of a cross, on a three-stepped calvary, ornamented with spirals ending with a fleur-de-lis, can be made out, although it is difficult to do so now. It is illustrated in detail in Inverness High School's booklet on their Abriachan project. There had been a chapel here long after the monks had gone and latterly it had been a preaching site.

Psalm 46

1. God is our refuge and our strength,
   in straights a present aid;
2. Therefore, although the earth remove,
   We will not be afraid:
Though hills amidst the seas be cast;
3. Though waters roaring make,
And troubled be; yea, though the hills
by swelling seas do shake.

The Psalms of David in metre.

St Colman became third abbot-bishop of Lindisfarne in Northumberland in AD 661, succeeding Saints Aidan and Finnan. Like them he had come from Ireland to become a monk at Iona and, like them, he travelled on various missionary journeys across Scotland. The settlement at Portmahomack (the Port of Colman or Colmac) on the Dornoch Firth, is dedicated to him. Colman still favoured Celtic practices regarding the dating of Easter and the tonsure of monks. When abbot of Lindisfarne he had the support of Osway, King of Northumbria but not of Osway's queen, Enfida, who came from Essex and favoured the Roman practices. In AD 664, Osway summoned the Synod of Whitby to settle these issues and Colman was defeated in debate. The Roman practices triumphed. Colman resigned, returned to Iona and then back to his native Ireland where he established several settlements in County Galway including one on the Aran Islands.

Colman's defeat at Whitby presaged the gradual decline of the Celtic Church, though in Ireland Roman authority was not fully established until the 12th century.

Opposite: Tarbat Old Parish Church or the Church of St Colman at Portmahomack, Easter Ross with the Dornoch Firth in the background. Beneath the present building, fragments of walls of earlier buildings, going back over 1000 years, have been unearthed. A grave marker recovered from the foundation of St Colman's Church in 1998 is similar to early grave markers at St Columba's monastery in Iona. The marker, illustrated opposite along with its reverse side, was recovered from the foundations of the church in 1998 and is now housed in the church along with many other fascinating and beautiful finds from the dig. These give a unique insight into life in the Pictish era.

Psalm 103

1. O thou my soul, bless God the Lord;
   and all that in me is
   Be stirred up his holy name
   to magnify and bless.
2. Bless, O my soul, the Lord thy God,
   and not forgetful be
   Of all his gracious benefits
   he hath bestowed on thee.

The Psalms of David in metre.

St Maelrubha, Ross-shire's foremost saint, was, like Columba, of royal Irish blood and a member of the monastery of Bangor in Ireland, one of the largest colleges of the Irish Church. Bangor means a monastic establishment with educational facilities attached. The Scottish equivalent is Banchory and two villages of that name, Banchory Ternan and Banchory Devenick, are found on the banks of the Dee in the North East of Scotland. The former is named for St Ternan who founded a famous seat of learning there. Maelrubha left Ireland for Scotland in AD 671 when he was twenty-nine years old. In AD 673, he founded the monastery of Applecross in Wester Ross, within sight of the Isles of Raasay and Skye. He later preached in Skye, notably near Broadford where Aisig Mourie (St Maelrubha's Ferry) marks the site of his church. The monastery in Applecross brought the Christian faith to the native Picts and for the monks it fulfilled the Irish ideal of white martyrdom – living in exile for the sake of their beliefs. Red martyrdom – death for their faith – came to many at the hands of the Vikings when their monastery was raided in AD 795. Applecross is known to this day as *'An Comraich'*, the Sanctuary. These early foundations offered the right of sanctuary for criminals. Such sanctuaries fell into disuse when a law was passed doing away with the imprisonment of debtors.

St Maelrubha continued to exercise his abbatical office for fifty-one years. In AD 722 he closed his labours, and his death is recorded by Tighearna thus: *"Maelrubha died a natural death in Applecross on the 21st day of April, being a Tuesday, his age being eighty years, three months and nineteen days."* Such is the Irish view of his history. Scottish authorities, while they also couple the memory and name of the saint with Applecross, differ materially regarding the date and manner of his death, as we shall see.

Opposite: The Abbot's Stone, the most obvious relic of what was believed to be a thriving monastery extending from the river to the hill behind Clachan Burial Ground and the old Parish Church of Applecross. This large unfinished carved stone, set in the ground to the left of the graveyard, originally marked the grave of Ruaraidh Mor MacAgon, Abbot of Applecross who, according to the Annals of Ulster, died as Abbot of Bangor in AD 801.

St John's Gospel Chapter 3

8. The wind bloweth where it listeth,
and thou hearest the sound thereof,
but canst not tell whence it cometh,
and whither it goeth:
so is everyone that is born of the Spirit.

Psalm 119

103. How sweet are thy words unto my taste!
yea, sweeter than honey to my mouth!
104. Through thy precepts I get understanding:
therefore I hate every false way.
105. Thy word is a lamp unto my feet,
and a light unto my path.

King James Authorised Version

Unlike the Irish annals, the *Breviary of Aberdeen* gives St Maelrubha's day as August 27th. Its compiler narrates that *"a body of pagan Norwegians, landing on the shores of Ross, slew Malrubius, and dragged his body into the thickets to be devoured by wild beasts."* It states that his martyrdom occurred at Urquhart, that on the spot where he suffered a wooden chapel was constructed, superseded by the parish church of Urquhart, and that his body was removed from this place and carried to Applecross. St Maelrubha is reputed to have founded settlements at Strathcarron, Contin and Ferintosh on the Black Isle. It was from his church at Ferintosh that he was fleeing from Danish or Norwegian pirates when he was killed. The brethren from the monastery of Applecross carried his body back to Applecross for burial. They stopped on the first night on an island in the River Blackwater, where the parish church of Contin now stands.

In the parish of Gairloch is Loch Maree, once called Loch Ewe, with Kinlochlochewe still at its head. Through time it has taken the name Maree from one of the islands called Innis Maree. The island which is situated in the middle of the loch has an ancient cemetery and it reputedly was once the residence of a good man called Maree, or Mourie or Maelrubha. A similar island in Loch Lomond, called Inch Murrin, was the dwelling place of St Mirin, who established his church in Paisley, west of Glasgow. A fair called Feil Maree used to be held in Contin on the last Wednesday of August and was latterly held in Dingwall.

Opposite: The fine pulpit in Clachan Church of Applecross. In the graveyard in which the church stands there is the ruin of a small rectangular chapel building. Beside it is a low mound which has always been called Cladh Maree. This mound is the site of a small rectangular building, which seems to have been no more than a cell. At a depth of two feet, there is a plain slab of stone which covers the stone kist in which was laid the mortal remains of Maelrubha, at full length, facing east. Fragments of carved stone, unearthed by the sexton, Kenneth Macrae FSA, and now housed in the church, are geologically native and the work unmistakably, according to the Society of Antiquarians, of the 8th century.

Psalm 103

8. The LORD is merciful and gracious,
slow to anger and plenteous in mercy.
9. He will not always chide.
neither will he keep his anger forever.
10. He hath not dealt with us after our sins;
nor rewarded us according to our iniquities.
11. For as the heaven is high above the earth,
so great is his mercy to them that fear him.
12. As far as the east is from the west,
so far hath he
removed our transgressions from us.

King James Authorised Version

Just as the people of Kintyre believe that St Columba sojourned there before he proceeded to Iona, so the people of Islay believe that St Maelrubha may well have sojourned on that island during the two years he spent in Scotland before establishing his monastery in Applecross. It appears that he was responsible for founding a Celtic monastic house there, an alternative to that of Columba.

Kilarrow (Kilmaelrubha or Kilmalruva or simply Kilruva) is the most southerly of his dedications. It is most likely that the church at Kilarrow was founded late in the 7th century or early in the 8th. The dedication is outwith the 'Columban' house. There is a strong tradition relating the church to a 'rival' house which points to specific activity by Maelrubha or his disciples.

The centre of population in the parish of Kilarrow moved from the original site of the monastic settlement to the village of Bowmore, a planned village created in 1768 to rehouse workers no longer involved in the running of the Islay estate. It was similar to several other such planned villages on the west coast of Scotland at that time. The inhabitants were expected to provide for themselves, especially through fishing.

Opposite: The parish church of Kilarrow now situated in Bowmore, in a commanding position on a hill at the top of the main street. It was so placed because David Campbell, laird of Islay, had been impressed by a similar church in Italy which he had visited as a young man. It was to be the focal point of the village and is known because of its shape as the 'Round Church'. It was reputedly made round in order that the devil would find no corners in which to hide. The Reverend Donald Caskie, a native of Bowmore and minister of the Scots Kirk in Paris when France was invaded by Germany in 1940, is laid to rest in the graveyard. Caskie, better known as *'The Tartan Pimpernel'*, stayed on in France to help organise the escape of British civilians from France but later became a vital link in the escape route for British and Allied servicemen from the south of France. As a result of this, he suffered greatly at the hands of the Nazis. He was awarded the OBE for his services, the medal for which is displayed in the church.

Psalm 103

13. Like as a father pitieth his children,
so the LORD pitieth them that fear him.
14. For he knoweth our frame; he remembereth that we are dust.
15. As for man, his days are as grass:
as a flower of the field, so he flourisheth.
16. For the wind passeth over it and it is gone;
and the place thereof shall know it no more.
17. But the mercy of the LORD is from everlasting to everlasting
upon them that fear him, and his righteousness
unto children's children.

King James Authorised Version.

One of the kings of Dalriada had a daughter who married an Irish chieftain, and gave birth to a son, Las or Laisren as he is known in Ireland. He returned to Ireland to be educated and before embarking on a pilgrimage to Rome he wished first to pass part of his life in relative solitude. He went to live as a hermit in a cave, on what is now called the Holy Isle, off the east coast of the island of Arran. There, like his master Jesus, he spent, in the fashion of his time, a period in the wilderness. Las had the common prefix *'mo'* meaning 'my' attached to his name and he became known as St Molas. Molaise, or Laisren, or Molas as he is more commonly known now, stayed long enough on Holy Island to be celebrated subsequently in the calendar of Scottish saints. He then made his journey to the 'holy city', Rome, to see the tombs of the apostles, to be received by the Pope and to study there for a period of years. He was consecrated a bishop by Pope Gregory and returned to Leinster, in Ireland, serving as Abbot of Leighlin until his death in AD 641.

Opposite: Holy Isle with St Molas' cave at the extreme left hand of the island seen from the east coast of Arran. St Molas' stone in the wall of Shiskine Church on the west of the island came from the graveyard in Clauchan Glen where it is believed St Molas was buried. The church in Shiskine is dedicated to him. It has been suggested, however, that the carving is not of St Molas but rather of an abbot of a later date of a settlement in neighbouring Kintyre where there were several monasteries of considerable renown. The Holy Isle's Gaelic name was Eilean Molaise, 'eilean' being 'island' and Molaise being Gaelic for Molas, pronounced *'Molash'*. This has been corrupted to Elmolaise and Lemolash to Lamlash which was the name of the island before 1830. It became the name of the village then developing on the opposite shore. The Holy Isle is now, significantly, owned by a Tibetan Buddhist community and used as a spiritual retreat for their own monks and nuns and as a place of contemplation for all faiths. The Tibetan Lama who founded the retreat was quoted as saying that *'Holy Isle has a powerful aura of spiritual energy.'*

Psalm 116

13. I will take the cup of salvation, and call upon the name of the LORD.
15. Precious in the sight of the LORD is the death of his saints.

St Luke's Gospel Chapter 22

19...... This is my body which is given for you:
this do in remembrance of me.
20..... This is the new testament in my blood,
which is shed for you.

King James Authorised Version.

When, in the 5th century, St Patrick arrived in Ireland, he found that the Celts there had long respected their women folk. Indeed the only members of that sex who deserved pity were the female slaves, who were treated simply as property. St Patrick wrote of those who were Christian that *"the Lord gave grace to many of His hand-maidens, for, although they were forbidden, they earnestly follow the example set them."* He, and St Brigid after him, worked hard to free them. Brigid was able to attain, in her lifetime, a unique position in her country; but then she herself was unique.

Brigid was born in AD 453. Her father was a pagan chieftain and her mother a Christian Pictish slave. Her mother taught her all she knew of the Christian faith and took her while she was still a small child to hear St Patrick preach. Brigid fell asleep, and on wakening entertained the congregation with a description of an exciting dream which she had had. St Patrick, who loved children, must have been the most appreciative member of her audience.

Brigid was generous to a fault and enraged her father, as it was often his goods that she gave away to the poor and needy. Exasperated with her behaviour he freed her and she made a present of that freedom to her mother, a bondswoman, who worked long and arduously in a dairy. Brigid took over most of the work from her. Her father next wished her to marry but she told him that she was already dedicated to God as were many others who were *'virgins in Christ'*. He acceded to her wishes and she took her vows as a nun. She gathered about her seven other nuns and hastened to the rescue of all those persecuted Christian women whose valuable lives were being wasted for want of a leader. She set up settlements as havens for the poor, the sick, and for tired travellers and also founded schools for children.

Long before she died in AD 523 legends about her were everywhere in the making, so greatly did Ireland rejoice in her existence. When taken literally, many of them seem incredible but it is well to remember that legends and myths often contain a higher degree of truth than do the bare bones of history.

Opposite: Stone and font from St Bride's Chapel at Kilbride graveyard in Lamlash, Isle of Arran. Removed from the graveyard in 1892 it is now located at the parish church of Kilbride in Lamlash. It almost certainly came from the 13th century monastery on Holy Isle, Eilean Molaise. It shows Christ passing into a chalice from which his blood pours to a supplicant. There is no known record of St Brigid having been in Scotland in person, but nevertheless she obviously had a tremendous influence in Scotland as well as in Ireland. There are many dedications to her, marked by many Kilbrides scattered across the length and breadth of Scotland.

St Mark's Gospel Chapter 15

34. My God, My God, why hast thou forsaken me?

Psalm 22

1. My God, My God, why hast thou forsaken me?
Why art thou so far from helping me
and from the words of my roaring?
19. But be thou not far from me O LORD:
O my strength, haste thee to help me.

St John's Gospel Chapter 15

12. This is my commandment,
That ye love one another, as I have loved you.
13. Greater love hath no man than this,
that a man lay down his life for his friends.

King James Authorised Version

St Blane was an uncle of St Molas and in turn his uncle was St Catan who gave his name to Kilchattan Bay in the south end of Bute. St Catan established the settlement in the 6th century at nearby Kingarth.

Bute was a major centre for early saints in which many ruined chapels and Celtic dedications bear witness. Tradition has it that Catan's sister had given birth to Blane out of wedlock and she and the infant were cast adrift in an oarless boat by the outraged Catan. The boat was driven ashore on the Ulster coast, where Blane spent the early years of his life before returning to Bute to be reunited with his uncle and to succeed him as abbot of the monastery which Catan had founded. St Blane then moved eastwards to Pictland and established a foundation beside the Allan Water which was to become Dunblane Cathedral.

St Brendan, the Navigator, is also commemorated in Bute and its inhabitants refer to themselves as Brandanes. Some scholars have argued that Bute is the *'Island of Delight'* mentioned in St Marnoc's *Navigato Sancti Brendani,* (the voyage of Saint Brendan). The story has been much embroidered, but it is possible that Brendan with his intrepid crew of pious monks reached the shores of Iceland, Greenland and even the mainland of North America. On one occasion, the Saint is said to have celebrated Easter on the back of an accommodating whale. The stretch of water separating Arran from Kintyre is called the Kilbrannan Sound in honour of the saint.

Opposite: St Blane's Norman Chapel and monastery, on Bute in the parish of Kingarth. Included is the 'cashel' or enclosing wall. There are also the foundations of an early Celtic chapel, a well, traces of the first monks' huts or cells, and an extensive cemetery which may include St Blane's grave. The chapel, situated as it is at the south west coast of Bute, faces the mountainous island of Arran and Holy Isle, St Molas' isle.

St John's Gospel Chapter 8

12. I am the light of the world:
he that followeth me shall not walk in darkness,
but shall have the light of life.

St John's Gospel Chapter 6

35. I am the bread of life:
he that cometh to me shall never hunger;
and he that believeth in me shall never thirst.

King James Authorised Version

St Duthac was born in Tain, Ross-shire, early in the 11th century and was educated there before going to Ireland for further study. The rest of his life was shared between the two countries. His reputation for personal sanctity grew quickly and he was said to be able to work great miracles. Many people came to seek his advice and experience his spiritual power. He is reputed to have died in Armagh in 1065, and earned the title of *'Chief confessor of Erin and Alba'*.

In the legends of St Duthac, as recorded in Bishop Elphinstone's *Aberdeen Breviary*, the following story is told. In a time of dearth, a landowner in Ross sent a loaf of bread to Duthac. It was made from dough rich in butter and sweetened with honey. These were precious ingredients and Duthac could not eat such food surrounded by poverty. He sent the loaf to another. So it continued through the day. Each who received the bread thought of another more deserving and by nightfall it had passed to the seventh, a poor man of the parish, who brought it once more as a gift to Duthac.

Duthac retraced *'the Circle of Bread'* from house to house, inviting each family to join him at the chapel. There he blessed the bread and broke each piece from the loaf as it was passed round. There was hardly a mouthful each and yet all were satisfied. One man carried away a few crumbs from the chapel and it was said that many sick people, whom no medicine could cure, were freed from their infirmities in the name of Christ, the Bread of Life, at the moment they tasted, or even smelled, the smallest fragment.

Opposite: The Collegiate Church of St Duthac in Tain, Ross-shire, probably completed by 1460. A Collegiate Church was one where a college of priests existed who would pray in perpetuity for the soul of the founder. Such was Duthac's prestige that his birthplace in Tain quickly became an important religious centre, its boundaries marked by four sanctuary crosses. In 1253 the saint's remains were returned to Tain and the shrine became a major place of pilgrimage, attracting not only local people but also the great, including King James IV who was especially devoted to the cult of St Duthac.

St Matthew's Gospel Chapter 5

43. Ye have heard that it hath been said,
Thou shalt love thy neighbour, and hate thine enemy.
44. But I say unto you, love your enemies,
bless them that curse you, do good to them that hate you,
and pray for them that despitefully use you, and persecute you;
45. That you may be children of your Father which is in heaven:
for he maketh the sun to rise on the evil and the good,
and sendeth the rain on the just and the unjust.

St Matthew's Gospel Chapter 6

9. Our Father which art in heaven, Hallowed be thy name.
10. Thy kingdom come. Thy will be done on earth as it is in heaven.
11. Give us this day our daily bread.
12. And forgive us our debts, as we forgive our debtors.
And lead us not unto temptation, but deliver us from evil:
For thine is the kingdom, the power, and the glory, for ever.
Amen.

St Luke's Gospel Chapter 14

34 .... Father forgive them, for they know not what they do.

King James Authorised Version.

Opposite: St Clement's Church, Rodel, Isle of Harris. Alexander Macleod, warrior chief of the Macleods of Harris and Dunvegan in Skye, rebuilt Rodel Church in 1528. He had a tomb built within it for himself. The tomb is ornately carved and amongst the images on it is one of St Clement, in the garb of a bishop. The church is most impressive and second only in size and prestige to Iona Abbey in the Western Isles. It is built on the site of a much older religious settlement. As with St Clement's Church in Dingwall, there is uncertainty with regard to which St Clement it is dedicated: Pope Clement, or Clement, Bishop of Dunblane, or the St Clement associated with Scandinavian sea-traders? In the early 16th century a free-standing cross was carved, in black amphibolite, and its surviving top section has been brought inside the church. The reverse shows a crucifixion with, most unusually, 'the hand of God' above.

Psalm 25

4. Shew me thy ways O LORD; teach me thy paths.
5. lead me in thy truth, and teach me;
for thou art the God of my salvation;
on thee do I wait all the day.
6. Remember, O LORD, thy tender mercies and thy lovingkindnesses,
for they have been of ever of old.

King James Authorised version.

St Margaret, Queen of Scotland, born in Hungary, was the granddaughter of the English king, Edward Ironside. When Edward died and the English people chose Canute as their ruler, Edward's infant sons were sent abroad to the protection of King Stephen of Hungary. Margaret, daughter of one of these sons, another Edward, came to England with her family and exiled father. It was hoped that her exiled father would succeed Edward the Confessor who had been king since the demise of Canute. Edward died on landing in England and his widow and children again found themselves living in dependence at court.

Margaret had a very strict religious upbringing. The change of country made little difference to her ordered life of prayer and work. About the same time another royal personage enjoyed the hospitality of the English Court. Malcolm, son of King Duncan of Scotland, was sent there for safety after the death of his father at the hands of Macbeth. There he may have met Margaret who was to become his queen.

In 1066 William the Conqueror became king of England, and Margaret's brother was advised to return with his sisters to Hungary for safety. They took ship but a fierce gale drove them northwards to seek shelter, firstly on the coast near Durham, then in a sheltered bay in Fife on the Firth of Forth, now called St Margaret's Hope. There Malcolm, now king of Scotland, hastened to meet and welcome her. Malcolm sought Margaret for his bride but her inclination and upbringing had prepared her for the cloister rather than the Crown. Malcolm was, however, a forceful and tempestuous monarch and suitor and after prolonged consideration Margaret yielded to his will.

The Anglo Saxon Chronicle tells the story: *"The Creator knew beforehand what he would have made of her for she was to increase God's praise in the land and direct the king from the erring path and bend him to a better way with his people."*

Opposite: Interior of the tiny St Margaret's Chapel, set high on the ramparts of Edinburgh Castle. In days of siege and war, as well as in days of plenty and peace, people have come here to worship God. The interior presents much the same appearance as it did in the days of David I who founded the Abbey of the Holy Rood in memory of his mother, Margaret. Restored in 1845 with the support of Queen Victoria, the five small windows were filled in with stained glass and later replaced, as we have them now, by the current beautiful windows. In 1942, the St Margaret's Chapel guild was started under the patronage of Princess Margaret. Members of the Guild, to this day, arrange that those with the name Margaret should supply and place flowers in the Chapel each week of the year.

St John's Gospel Chapter 14

I am the way, the truth, and the life:
no man cometh to the Father; but by me.
7. If ye had known me, ye should have known my Father also:
and from henceforth ye know him and have seen him.

St Mark's Gospel Chapter 10

14.. Suffer the little children to come unto me and forbid them not:
for of such is the kingdom of God.
15. Verily I say unto you, Whosoever shall not receive
the kingdom of God as a little child, he shall not enter therein.

King James Authorised version.

Margaret continued to live an ordered life of prayer and work, as advocated by St Benedict and well summed up by St Teresa *"to give our Lord perfect service Martha and Mary must combine."* The Benedictine, Lancfranc (scholar, saint and Archbishop of Canterbury), had reorganised the church in England, and with his help and friendship Queen Margaret did likewise with the church in Scotland. She won over the hearts of her and her husband's subjects who allowed themselves to be moulded by her, seeing the beginnings of the blend of Celt and Saxon which continues to this day. Zealous as she was for her own Roman Catholic faith, she showed no hostility to the Church founded by St Columba. It was under her influence and that of her sons, King David I in particular, that the Scottish church ceased to have a narrowly Celtic aspect and conformed to the wider Christian ethic of Europe.

Five hundred years before Columba arrived on these shores the Christian Church had been established, and by the end of the first century AD the third Bishop of Rome, St Clement, martyred. Now, five hundred years after St Columba, St Margaret effectively, if necessarily, presided over the demise of Columba's Celtic Church. Five hundred years later that same Roman Catholic Church, which replaced the Celtic Church, fell on difficult times and the Reformation heralded the birth of the Protestant Church in Scotland, and at a later date Presbyterianism. Five hundred years later, in the 21st century it may be that some radical form of change is imminent as support for organised religion is at an all-time low. Many are deeply concerned and fear that the Church may soon cease to exist altogether, but it may be worth noting that Scotland has gone down this road before. A former editor of the Church of Scotland's magazine *Life and Work*, R D Kernohan has written: *"A time will come, no one knows when, for the completion of all things. Meanwhile faith, hope, and love remain. The future is His, not ours. We should work for the future of our Church and spend less time worrying about it."*

Opposite: Memorial window in St Clement's Church, Dingwall, for a noted family in the burgh. Depicting St Columba and St Margaret it was created by stained glass artist Roland Mitton of Livingston.

Psalm 23

1. The Lord's my shepherd, I'll not want.
2. He makes me down to lie
In pastures green : he leadeth me the quiet waters by.
3. My soul he doth restore again :
and me to walk doth make
Within the paths of righteousness,
ev'n for his own name's sake.

4. Yea, though I walk in death's dark vale,
yet will I fear none ill :
For thou art with me ;
and thy rod and staff me comfort still.
5. My table thou hast furnished
in presence of my foes ;
My head thou dost with oil anoint,
and my cup overflows.

6. Goodness and mercy all my life
shall surely follow me :
And in God's house for evermore
my dwelling-place shall be.

The Psalms of David in metre

St John's Gospel Chapter 10

11. I am the good shepherd:
the good shepherd giveth his life for the sheep.

27. My sheep hear my voice,
and I know them and they follow me:
28. And I give unto them eternal life;
and they shall never perish.
neither shall any man pluck them out of my hand.

St John's Gospel Chapter 14

27. Peace I leave with you,
my peace I give unto you:
not as the world giveth, give I unto you.
Let not your heart be troubled,
neither let it be afraid.

St John's Gospel Chapter 20

29.....because thou hast seen me thou hast believed:
blessed are they that have not seen,
and yet have believed.

St John's Gospel Chapter 21

17....., lovest thou me?
...., Feed my sheep.

King James Authorised Version.

Psalm 24.

7. Ye gates lift up your heads on high;
ye doors that last for aye,
Be lifted up that so the King of glory enter may.
8. But who of glory is the King?
The mighty Lord is this;
Ev'n that same Lord, that great in might
and strong in battle is.

9. Ye gates, lift up your heads; ye doors,
doors that do last for aye,
Be lifted up, that so the King of glory enter may.
10. But who is he that is the King of glory? who is this?
The Lord of hosts, and none but he,
the King of glory is.

The Psalms of David in metre

St Matthew's Gospel Chapter 26

64.... Hereafter ye shall see the Son of man
sitting on the right hand of power,
and coming in the clouds of heaven.

Psalm 46.

10. Be still and know that I am God :
I will be exalted among the heathen, I will be exalted in the earth.

King James Authorised Version

Opposite: Traigh an t-suidhe, at the northernmost point of Iona. Saint Columba reputedly visited this spot often: resting, meditating, and simply enjoying the view. To the North West the isles of Coll and Tiree can be discerned. To the North Rum and, on a clear day, the Cuillin of Skye are visible, while in the North East lies the island of Mull.

Opposite: Map showing various locations, referred to in the text, which are associated with Scotland's saints. On the section showing part of Northern Ireland, appears Derry, where Columba built his first monastery. His days there were a treasured memory throughout his life. At Downpatrick, in Northern Ireland, St Patrick and St Brigid were buried.

When the Vikings raided Iona, precious articles and manuscripts were taken to Ireland to the monasteries of Kells and Durrow for safe keeping. The accompanying illuminated capital letters, decoration and portrait of St Matthew are taken from the *Book of Kells.*

St Columba's birthplace in Donegal, and the monasteries of Kells, Durrow, Clonard, Clonmacnoise and Leighlin are all in Southern Ireland. Lindisfarne, Durham and Whitby, all mentioned in the text, are on the North East coast of England.

Harris
Rodell
Ross-shire
Portmahomack
Tain
Moray Firth
Loch Maree
Contin
Dingwall
Black Isle
Rosemarkie
Skye
Raasay
Applecross
Abriachan
Inverness
Aberdeenshire
The Minch
Castle
Urquhart
Loch Ness
River Dee
Aberdeen
Banchory
Achnacarry
Fort William
Iona
Mull
Lismore
Oban
Dundee
Perth
Strathearn
St Andrews
Dunning
Colonsay
Oronsay
Dunblane
Stirling
Fife
Cultross
Firth of Forth
Dalriada
Drymen
Loch Lomond
Dumbarton
St Margaret's Hope
Islay
Kilarrow
Bute
Strathclyde
Glasgow
Edinburgh
Paisley
River Clyde
Atlantic
Ocean
Kildalton
St Blane's Chapel
Arran
Shiskine
Lamlash
Holy Isle
Kintyre
Southend
Firth of
Clyde
Scotland
Derry
Ulster
Galloway
Hadrian's
Wall
Ireland
Roman
Britain
Belfast Loch
Bangor
Whithorn
Solway Firth
Armagh
Downpatrick
Isle of Whithorn

FURTHER READING

Huyshe, Wentworth: The Life of Saint Columba by Saint Adamnan, London.
Leatham, Diana: They Built on Rock, Glasgow, 1948.
Wallace, Martin: A Little Book of Celtic Saints, Belfast, 1995.
Smith, Donald: Celtic Travellers, The Stationery Office, Edinburgh, 1997.
Carver, Martin: Surviving in Symbols, Historic Scotland, Edinburgh, 1999.
Carver, Martin: Discovery at Tarbat, University of York, 1998.
Campbell, Ewan: Saints and Sea Kings, Historic Scotland, Edinburgh, 1999
Ritchie, Anne and Fisher, Ian: Iona Abbey and Nunnery, Historic Scotland, 2001.
MacArthur, Mairi: Iona, Colin Baxter Photography Grantown-on-Spey, 1999.
Official Guide: St Serf's, Dunning and the Dupplin Cross, Historic Scotland.
Tabraham, Chris: Urquhart Castle, Loch Ness, Historic Scotland, 2002.
Newton, Norman: Islay, Devon, 1988.
Maclellan, Robert (Revised by Norman Newton): Arran, Devon, 1995.
Kenny, Colum: Molaise, Abbot of Leighlin and Holy Island, County Mayo, 1998
Stewart, Katharine: A School in the Hills, Edinburgh, 1996.
Alston, David: Ross and Cromarty, Edinburgh, 1999.
A'Chomraich (Applecross) The Sanctuary, A Glimpse of History, Applecross Historical Society.
Lawson, Bill: St Clement's Church at Rodel, Stornoway, 1991.
Robertson, Charles (Editor): St Margaret, Queen of Scotland, Edinburgh, 1994.

ACKNOWLEDGEMENTS

Grateful thanks to David and Sandra Macdonald of Dingwall: David for making available researched material on St Clement originally published in his book *St Clement's Looks Back*; Sandra for material on St Maelrubha and on her native Applecross. The draft history for A'Chromaich – The Sanctuary was written by the late Kenneth MacRae FSA Scot. of Camustiel, who was Sandra's father.

Grateful thanks also to Dr Ronald Fyfe of Northern College of Education, Aberdeen, for valuable advice concerning the compilation of this book.

Thanks also to Mr and Mrs MacKechnie, Dingwall, for advice concerning Gaelic translations.

Thanks also to my son, William, and to Miss Marilyn Ferguson for valuable assistance on the IT front.

Opposite: Kildalton High Cross in Islay is one of the finest High Crosses in Scotland. It was carved about AD 800, probably by a sculptor from Iona, from the local blue stone. The Biblical scenes on the front include the Virgin and Child and David and the lion, while on the back are animals and carved bosses. The name 'Kildalton' meaning 'the church of the foster child or disciple' probably refers to St John the Evangelist, the beloved disciple.

Although no surface traces remain, there was undoubtedly a monastic foundation at Kildalton. In all probability it came under the sphere of influence of the 'Columban' Church. The ruined medieval church was probably built in the late 12th or early 13th century under the patronage of the Lord of the Isles.